馬丁·路德·金

Heroes and Role Models | Non-Fiction Series

Copyright © 2022 by Level Learning, INC. and Washington Yu Ying PCS™
Original and Edited Text Copyright © 2022 by Washington Yu Ying PCS™

All rights reserved. No part of this book in whole or part may be reproduced without written permission from the publisher.

Published by Level Learning, INC.
Content Contributors:
Washington Yu Ying PCS™ - Teng Shen, Pearl Zao He You
Level Learning - Jingyao Qi

Illustrations by: Matt Austin

Leveling classification based on Level Learning standard.
For full description, visit www.levellearning.com

ISBN 978-1-64040-049-8
Traditional Chinese Edition

About Level Learning:

Level Learning provides a literacy focused curriculum specifically designed for K-12 Chinese as a Second Language classrooms. Our program offers 20 levels of specific and detailed objectives, leveled texts and passages, mastery-based online assessment, and analytics to enable data-driven instruction. Level Learning reading curriculum for both literature and informational text emphasize grammar and comprehension skills to help teachers develop confident and independent Chinese language readers. The non-fiction series of books are specifically designed to support our informational text course based on multiple national standards. To learn more about our entire offering, visit www.levellearning.com.

About Washington Yu Ying PCS™:

Washington Yu Ying PCS is a Mandarin English dual language immersion International Baccalaureate (IB) World school. Yu Ying's mission is to inspire and prepare young people to create a better world by challenging them to reach their full potential in a nurturing Chinese/English educational environment. Yu Ying's comprehensive IB, dual immersion curriculum equips students with global competencies for success in the real world. As a leader in immersion education, Yu Ying is determined to advance Chinese language programs and global citizenry education by helping other schools create and strengthen their Chinese programs. For more information, email: products@washingtonyuying.org

馬丁·路德·金出生在美國的一個非洲裔家庭。

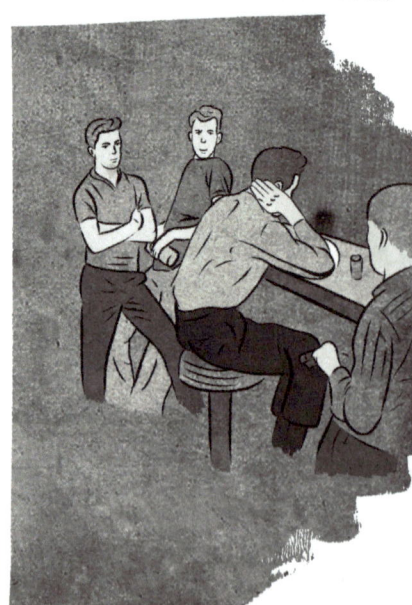

在他小時候，非洲裔不能去白人的商店買東西;非洲裔不能去白人的飯店吃飯;非洲裔也不能去白人的學校學習。

馬丁希望有一天，世界上所有的人都是平等的。

長大以後，馬丁到處演講，組織遊行。他用非暴力的方式告訴人們，什麼是公平和平等。

那時，在公交車上，白人可以坐在前排，非洲裔只能坐後排。一個非洲裔女子因為**拒絕**給白人讓座，被警察抓走了。

馬丁知道後，馬上組織了抗議遊行。在之後的一年多裡，很多人都拒絕坐公交車。後來，非洲裔在公交車上可以自由地選擇座位。

馬丁做過很多次演講，其中最著名的是「我有一個夢想」。1963年8月28日，25萬不同膚色、不同種族的人來到華盛頓紀念碑前。馬丁告訴全世界他有一個夢想，他希望不同種族的人能平等地生活。

馬丁的努力推動了美國的種族平等。 1964年,馬丁得到了「諾貝爾和平獎」。

為了紀念馬丁·路德·金作出的貢獻，每年一月的第三個星期一被定為「馬丁·路德·金日」。

Glossary

	Pinyin	English Definition
非洲裔	fēi zhōu yì	African descent
平等	píng děng	fair, equal
演講	yǎn jiǎng	speech
組織	zǔ zhī	to organize
遊行	yóu xíng	parade
非暴力	fēi bào lì	non-violent
公平	gōng píng	fairness
拒絕	jù jué	to refuse
抗議	kàng yì	protest
自由	zì yóu	free
種族	zhǒng zú	race
華盛頓	huá shèng dùn	Washington
紀念碑	jì niàn bēi	monument
推動	tuī dòng	to promote
諾貝爾和平獎	nuò bèi ěr hé píng jiǎng	Nobel Peace Prize

	Pinyin	English Definition
紀念	jì niàn	to commemorate
貢獻	gòng xiàn	contribution

www.ingramcontent.com/pod-product-compliance
Lightning Source LLC
Chambersburg PA
CBHW041224070526
44584CB00001B/78